GET RETIREMENT READY

5 STEPS TO A SECURE RETIREMENT

TONY DRAKE, CFP®

Tony Drake is registered as an Investment Advisor Representative and is a licensed insurance agent. Drake & Associates, LLC is an independent financial services firm that helps individuals create retirement strategies using a variety of investment and insurance products to custom suit their needs and objectives.

The contents of this book are provided for informational purposes only and are not intended to serve as the basis for any financial decisions. Any tax, legal, or estate planning information is general in nature. It should not be construed as legal or tax advice. Always consult an attorney or tax professional regarding the applicability of this information to your unique situation.

Information presented is believed to be factual and up to date, but we do not guarantee its accuracy, and it should not be regarded as a complete analysis of the subjects discussed. All expressions of opinion are those of the author as of the date of publication and are subject to change. Content should not be construed as personalized investment advice, nor should it be interpreted as an offer to buy or sell any securities mentioned. A financial advisor should be consulted before implementing any of the strategies presented.

Investing involves risk, including the potential loss of principal. No investment strategy can guarantee a profit or protect against loss in periods of declining values. Any references to protection benefits or guaranteed/lifetime income streams refer only to fixed insurance products, not securities or investment products. Insurance and annuity product guarantees are backed by the financial strength and claims-paying ability of the issuing insurance company.

Any names used in the examples in this book are hypothetical only and do not represent actual clients.

Get Retirement-Ready

Copyright © 2022, Tony Drake

Published in the United States of America

220203-02039

ISBN 9798848005134

No parts of this publication may be reproduced without correct attribution to the author of this book.

Table of Contents

Introduction

Born and raised in Wisconsin to incredible parents, I was part of your typical middle-class, American family. Mom worked on a factory line, building small engines, and Dad welded car frames. Both of my parents spent their lives in the service of others. They were role models for me and highlighted what a prosperous, hard-earned future could look like. But it wasn't that simple.

Through a series of bad decisions, I found myself at twenty years old, having forgotten their guidance and losing everything. At my lowest point, I became a full-time, single parent and upside down over $40,000 in credit card debt!

A wake-up call was past due, and through the intervention of a close friend, I finally listened. Time to wake up, Tony.

It became clear to me, all those decades ago, that to create a better life for my daughter, any future children, myself, and our community—dramatic change was needed. What's the saying? Nothing changes if nothing changes.

My early twenties served as an eventual calling to follow a passion for finance and to enter the financial services arena. I had made mistakes—a lot of them. But getting my own finances and life in order also meant I was now equipped to help others do the same. I often think about those with hopes and dreams, but no plans or actions—because decades ago, that was me.

But today, I get to fill my days visiting with people from all walks of life; different backgrounds, beliefs, influences, and perceptions. What I've learned is many of us share similar goals (maybe just different ways of approaching them). Peace of mind, freedom, health, family, and a pursuit of happiness are vital to all of us.

Mom and Dad taught me that through their hard work and sacrifices. I'm now blessed to realize their wisdom and use what I've learned over the years to share it with others.

Many people planning for retirement will ask me, "Do I have enough money? Will I be okay?" What they're really asking is, "Will I have the income I need to handle all the hurdles that come up in retirement?"

These questions and concerns arise from so many talking heads we see on TV, hear on the radio, and watch on YouTube. Many of these "advisors" spout the "flavor of the week" regarding investments and creating income in retirement. Some may be sound, but many can be very high risk for someone nearing or currently in retirement.

Additionally, many retirees have addressed retirement investments by socking away large amounts of their money into pre-tax retirement accounts like a 401(k), 403(b), 457, TSPs, Traditional IRAs, the list goes on and on. Still, in my experience, many have not addressed the five crucial areas that I believe need attention and planning to have a successful and enjoyable retirement.

It is important to have a plan to save money for retirement, but we believe it is crucial to also have a plan leading to and after retirement.

What does this look like?

We call it the Retirement-Ready Roadmap. This roadmap is designed to help you understand the important parts of a successful retirement plan. We believe that if this process is followed, it can lead to greater financial confidence in retirement. After a fun day with your friends, family, and grandkids, retirement isn't just about knowing your retirement money will be there when you need it, but also in having a plan for when and where to pull the money from.

I hope this book helps inspire you to take control of your financial plan. You deserve a comprehensive financial and income plan personalized to your specific future hopes and dreams for yourself and your heirs.

To your best retirement,

Tony Drake

CHAPTER 1

Readying for Retirement

My philosophy's changed a bit over the years. Being a number and data nerd, when I started, I was so focused on the investments and trying to help people get everything from their investments. I've since learned that is an important *part* of the retirement plan, but it's not *the* whole plan.

I started my business in 2002. I often think about two of my heroes, Grandma and Grandpa, children of the depression, great savers, and conservative spenders. Due to the formative experience in their childhood, they were EXTREMELY conservative investors. Even though Grandpa was a PhD in economics, he spent fifty years talking about the next Great Depression. I wonder if they had invested and planned a little more appropriately, what life they might have had? My experience with them has been another driving force in my career.

Over the years, I've learned that crossing the bridge into retirement can be very emotional. It's very difficult for some people to suddenly start taking money out of the accounts they have invested in for so long. The risk of loss becomes a lot scarier.

Having a good retirement plan can help provide confidence. Many of us ask some version of the question, "Do I have enough money? Am I going to be okay?" It's common to be concerned about outliving assets. People want to know they'll be able to live the retirement of their dreams, which includes that bucket list of all the things they want to do.

"Am I going to have the money, the resources, and the assets to do that? Can my retirement survive inflation, market volatility, rising taxes, and healthcare expenses—all these big hurdles that I may end up facing in retirement?"

Having a retirement plan that has been designed to address these various risks could help bring a greater sense of calmness to your retirement. You may be able to shift beyond thinking about the money, worrying about whether you have enough to enjoy your retirement years. Maybe you aim to spend it all, pass it all on, or a combination of the two. What are those things that you've spent decades saving and working for?

What Is Often Overlooked?

We've had the opportunity to meet thousands of different families over the years, and, in our experience, the root cause of many issues generally boils down to a lack of a comprehensive plan. We address this with one simple-to-understand document that defines:

- How am I invested?

- Where is my income coming from? From what accounts and what order?

- How do I deal with healthcare?

- How might tax planning strategies help reduce my taxes over the decades in retirement?

- What is the plan for my family's continuity and succession?

Creating a plan up front isn't enough, though. The planning must be ongoing.

Your plan should include mid-course corrections. It should contain ebbs and flows. There are always opportunities for adaptation. It's not the direction of the wind; it's the set of the sail!

How does your plan adapt to new tax laws in varying market environments? There are generally some sectors or some market areas that we can take advantage of. What tax strategies have you implemented? We need a plan that can change and adapt as your retirement changes. Many people come to us worrying about having enough money. What they're really asking me is about income. Whether they realize it or not, they're asking, "Am I going to have the income to survive all these things?"

If the market is down 20, 30, or 40 percent, you still want to be able to do the fun stuff. You don't want to be sitting there saying, "Can I go on my trip? Can I visit the grandkids? Can I do the various things that I've dreamed about?" You want to know that your plan has accounted for these things.

In many of my public speaking engagements, financial seminars, television news appearances, or on my radio show, I'll ask the question, "How many of you feel that you have a retirement and income plan—with a caveat—that you understand?" Very few hands go up.

It's shocking to me. Often, these people are within a couple of years of retirement, or already retired, and still don't have a plan they understand. The part of my job that I love the most is demystifying retirement planning with my clients. When I'm sitting in the office or on a virtual call with someone, and we put a plan together, we can display very complicated concepts in a simple manner. People often cry or are excited or overjoyed because they see it for the first time. Being a part of that process with so many families is truly a gift and something I love about the career that I've chosen.

I love helping people work through some of their economical concerns. We've met with a lot of people who don't understand their plan. We hear the horror stories of people who don't have enough, and they have to work longer.

Some people have too much risk in their portfolio. When volatility hits, whether it's through a pandemic, a housing bubble, or something else, they are often struck with overwhelming concern. They tend to hit the panic button at the worst point, when the market's at the bottom, because they don't have a comprehensive plan that's been tested to help manage these types of risks. They think, "I can't afford to lose anymore," instead of knowing, "My plan's been tested for market volatility, and I think that I'm going to be okay."

On the other hand, some people work too long because they're so afraid of being able to take out their money. They're so afraid that they can't answer that question, "Do I have enough money? Am I going to be okay?" They end up working later in life and miss out on wonderful years of retirement they can never get back.

Children of the Depression

As I mentioned earlier, my grandparents are probably one of the best examples of this frugal anxiety. Grandpa was a World War II Navy vet. When he got back from World War II, he got a PhD in economics. Back then, he worked as a professor, and every seven years, he'd get to take a sabbatical. He'd pack the family up, they'd move to another country, and he would write a book about the economics in that area. Grandma would learn a language in weeks. She was brilliant.

I can't imagine what that was like to grow up during the depression, not knowing if you would have your next meal or even a consistent place to live. Though Grandpa was, quite literally, a PhD in economics, he spent fifty years talking about the next depression being right around the corner. He hardly invested, with the exception of CDs and a few very conservative investments. Because my grandparents were conservative spenders, this fear of investment didn't affect their lives a whole lot. Still, I can only imagine if they'd had a more diversified portfolio of investments, one tested for their risk tolerance, what they could have potentially saved and how they could have enjoyed those savings in retirement. I think it probably cost them a lot because their financially unstable childhood was so formative.

Questions to Ask Yourself

There are a couple of questions you might want to think about.

- Has my retirement plan been tested for the good and bad times?

- If there is a market correction or housing crisis where the market drops, say, 50 percent, do I know my plan will work? Can I continue to live the retirement of my dreams, or does that concern cause me to say, "I should have worked longer," or "I have to forgo those fun things"?

I've learned an important lesson: ***Losses hurt more than gains feel good.*** For many retirees, if their portfolio goes up 25 percent, they won't spend any more than they were before. They don't usually have a very big emotional reaction. They're happy, but they're not going to change their current spending.

If they lose 20, 30, 40 percent, now they're saying, "Should I have kept working? Should I go on vacation? Should I help the grandkids the way I want to? Can I do some of these things that I've dreamed about?"

Maybe you're telling yourself, "I don't have a plan that's been tested for these kinds of changes. I don't feel confident, so I am still working," or "I'm in retirement, worried about affording what I want to do. I feel paralyzed, so I'm not spending any money." That could be a tragedy.

Maybe you wait until later in life to retire and now this hurts, that hurts, you're sick, you can't physically travel, and are missing out on the plans and trips you dreamed about. You may have missed an opportunity because fear paralyzed you.

A great question to ask yourself is, do you have the confidence that when major market corrections inevitably occur, your retirement will be okay?

My Encouragement to You

My biggest encouragement to people entering or nearing retirement is that it's possible. It can feel very scary. It can feel very emotional, but when preparing your Retirement-Ready Roadmap, a good professional should be able to help walk you through these steps.

There are five unique areas that we believe need to be addressed, and each of these areas can be planned for. That's the foundation of the Retirement-Ready Roadmap! We believe most of the concerns that are specific and unique to your family can be addressed in this plan.

It can be done. If you are saying, "Money, investments … that's not my deal. I was a good saver. I did what I was supposed to do. I took money out of every check, and I put it away, but I don't understand this," there are very simple ways to create plans that can help put you at ease. Don't feel overwhelmed. It is a process, but you can accomplish it and be successful in this process!

Your Retirement-Ready Roadmap

Why do we feel that a Retirement-Ready Roadmap is so essential for retirement? We've met so many families over the years that don't have a clear picture of what retirement is. There are so many questions that come along:

- Where is my income coming from?

- From what accounts?

- In what order?

- How long will that income last?

Although every family's unique, and your plan will be unique, we have found five key areas that we believe have to be addressed in everyone's retirement plan. Often, when we meet new families, I'll go through these five areas, and I'll say, "Why don't you rate yourself in the following areas? 1 being not prepared at all, 10 being I got this licked. No 7s allowed."

If you would like to rate yourself, visit www.retirementreadyroadmap.com/RateMyself

---

Investments

The first area is investments. Many folks come to us and feel like they have a good grasp of their investments. Sometimes that's the case. Sometimes they have some false hope in this area. This is what a lot of people think about as their whole retirement plan. In reality, this is part of the plan, but not "the plan" itself.

Income

The next area is income, and this is an area where people often rate themselves fairly low. They don't know which account their money is coming from and in what order. They don't always understand that taking income in the right order can possibly add years to the longevity of their portfolio.

Many retirees also fail to understand the sequence of return risk. This concept is fairly simple: losses early in retirement can be much more impactful on the longevity of your portfolio than losses later in retirement. If not planned for, this can dramatically reduce the lifespan of your money. We must understand that for most retirees, the first decade-plus is a very vulnerable time.

Healthcare

The next area is healthcare. Many of us have concerns about health and wellness, family continuity, or rising healthcare costs. You have all these different parts that can be so confusing. Having someone who can help you walk through that is important.

Tax Strategies

The next area is tax planning strategies. This is another area where, when I ask folks to rate themselves; many rate themselves very low, often between 1 and 3. You've called your advisor, and they have said what? You ask a tax question, and they say, "Great question. Call the accountant. I'm not an accountant."

I'm also not an accountant, but I believe that tax strategies might be one of the single best areas that could help increase the longevity of your portfolio. It's simple: if you're paying less to Uncle Sam, you don't have to take out as much, and your money can last longer. Implementing tax-efficient strategies, especially early in retirement, can have a big impact on your entire retirement. It's not necessarily about the size of your accounts. It really boils down to, "How much do I get to keep, and how much goes to Uncle Sam?"

We find that some financial advisors focus primarily on investments. They don't always think much about the taxes or all five of these areas working together. Tax planning strategies are a big area that we believe is not addressed in most retirement plans.

Family

The last area is family. Most of the folks we meet with are coming in saying, "Look, Tony, I want to make sure my spouse is okay. I want to make sure my kids are taken care of. I don't want it to be a hassle for them when something happens to me. I want this family secure."

Many of us have stuck large amounts of money away in tax-deferred accounts (these are typically retirement accounts through an employer where we invested pre-tax), but these accounts can be what some call a "ticking tax time bomb" either for you or for your non-spousal beneficiaries. Some laws have changed in recent years, and some beneficiaries have to cash certain inherited retirement accounts out within ten years. That could move them into a higher tax bracket. It's important to ensure legal documents and tax strategies are in place to pass our money onto our loved ones in the most tax-efficient manner. After all, after saving, investing, and planning so well, do you really want Uncle Sam to the be largest beneficiary?

You need to get these five areas on your Retirement-Ready Roadmap working together. The roadmap is one of the reasons at my firm, we have accountants who do tax returns for our clients. We'll bring the accountants right into the room when we discuss tax strategies and issues. We have a health insurance agent who can help you sort through long-term care and Medicare Supplements and Advantage. We have an elder law attorney on sight helping with wills, trusts, and powers of attorney.

We can bring together all the professionals in the room, so when you call in, you don't hear, "Hey, that's not my job. Call someone else." We think this team ought to be working together for you, and that's why we feel it's so important to have that comprehensive Retirement-Ready Roadmap that addresses all five areas.

We focus on "One Plan, One Coach," coordinating all of the professionals to help guide you through the retirement of your dreams!

Tom and Suzanne's Story

Tom and Suzanne are a fantastic couple we met several years ago, self-traders. Like so many folks, they handled their own investments without an advisor. They heard me speak at an engagement and decided to come in for a complimentary consultation. While they hadn't accounted for many of the five areas in their own financial planning, frankly, their investments weren't bad.

But they had not accounted for an income plan and what impacts inflation would have on that. They hadn't accounted for any tax strategies that could potentially improve their plan. They had no plan to address healthcare, their longevity, well-being, or how to deal with rising healthcare costs. There was also no plan for family continuity.

We believed they needed a five-part plan, and they were only addressing one part. I liken that to a stool that needs five legs but only has one. The five-legged stool is comfy and rock solid. A one-legged stool is wobbly and nerve-racking because it's almost impossible to balance.

For clients who are lacking in some areas of planning, a customized Retirement-Ready Roadmap could potentially make substantial improvements that might add a lot of dollars to the longevity of their plan. It can help lead to more money to spend and leave for children and grandchildren. It could even help minimize the taxes paid on an inheritance.

We've seen this with many families. Beyond the dollars and cents is an understanding on how this works together, knowing it's been tested to help you weather both the good and bad times. That knowledge is what helps you to take out and spend money without worrying, "Am I going to outlive my money?"

A Tax Dilemma

Tom and Suzanne had a real income tax dilemma that they had not addressed. We walked through a simple strategy where we showed them what they could be facing in retirement from an income tax perspective. Like most retirees, they had saved most of their money in their retirement accounts—401(k), 403(b), 457 and traditional IRAs—so they had this large pending tax liability that was growing every year. They weren't aware there are strategic Roth conversions that can allow people to take pre-tax dollars and convert them, paying the taxes on converted funds now to enjoy tax-free benefits later.

Assuming the rules are followed, that money can grow income tax-free, come out tax-free, and be passed on to loved ones income tax-free. Those two words, "tax-free," sure have a nice ring to them.

These types of conversions can sometimes have a big impact on the taxation of other income sources and on the amount that's left for loved ones to inherit with less of a tax burden.

The combination of different strategies we'll get into in the following chapters include creating a Social Security strategy, balancing risk to help generate guaranteed lifetime income, implementing a strategic Roth conversion or integration strategy, establishing a trust for children, and walking through the Medicare planning process.

When you have all of these strategies working successfully together in concert, they can have a positive impact on your life.

Questions to Ask Yourself

- Do you have a retirement and income plan that you understand?

- Do you understand exactly where your income's coming from: what accounts and in what order?

- Do you understand how to deal with market downturns?

- Do you understand how your plan addresses rising taxes? We look at tax rates historically, and they're relatively low right now. How are you then going to deal with potentially rising taxes?

- How can you address healthcare?

- How can you make sure your family is going to be okay?

If you are clear on the questions above, you're probably in great shape. However, many of us are not and need help in some of these areas.

CHAPTER 3

Investments & Risk

When we discuss investments, we generalize a little bit. Most of the families who come in to our office initially have all of their money, or a good majority of it, in their 401(k) or some employer-sponsored retirement plan, and they're concentrating on what I call the risk bucket. They often have no risk diversification. Everything is invested in mutual funds, stocks, bonds, and ETFs. They're at a high-risk level, concerned that it's going to hurt if the market corrects. As mentioned, data shows that losses earlier in retirement can be more impactful than losses later in retirement.

As you're zooming in on that first decade in retirement, when you're often more vulnerable. You're exposed to market losses, and some people haven't thought about them. A lot of investors aren't even really looking at it. They're just thinking, "Ah, I'll keep putting money in. I don't have to touch that money," which is a great philosophy—a great theory—when you're in your thirties and forties, still working, and won't need the money for many decades. However, most families we meet have a risk level that we think is too high. We have a very simple process for risk assessment where we use a program that asks clients a series of questions to provide an emotional risk number.

We're going to focus a little bit on the downside for a moment. You answer these questions, and you're assigned a risk number from 1 to 99. A 1 means, "I have everything safe at the bank or under my mattress. I don't care about inflation risk; I don't care about losing the purchasing power of my dollars. I don't want to lose." Meanwhile, 99 means you're willing to take on any amount of risk.

For example, in Tom and Suzanne's case, they were emotionally at a score of 40, which is defined as conservative. When we analyzed their portfolio, they were invested at a score of 78, which would define them as risk-takers. We help determine your comfort level when it comes to risk, then we compare and ask, "Okay, based on what you're comfortable with, how far down would the market need to be before you hit the panic button potentially making a big mistake: panicking and selling out at the bottom?"

Tom and Suzanne were taking nearly double the risk they were emotionally comfortable with, and we see this almost every day. This instance begs the question: Why are you taking double the risk? I get the same answer nine times out of ten. People will say either, "I had no idea," or they'll say, "If I told my advisor once, I've told them 100 times. I wanted a more conservative portfolio."

Risk Is Riskier as You Age

Some people don't understand the risk they're taking, and they don't understand the impact of that risk. Warren Buffett has a great quote: "Why take a risk that you don't need?"

I've met many families that statistically have the income they need to live a great retirement. Yet they are taking risk where they might lose 30, 40, even 50 percent. These types of dramatic losses could change the longevity of their dollars, in some cases causing them to run out of money entirely. If your retirement can be successful with a more conservative portfolio, why take unnecessary risk?

Think about it. You've already won the retirement income game. You've made it to that retirement age you've been dreaming about. You've analyzed it. You have enough money. Why take risk that might change the answer to, "Do I have enough money?" Many families come in with a basket of unnecessarily risky investments that they haven't diversified into different risk buckets.

Different Kinds of Risk

It's important to have a balanced approach. There's no one right answer for everybody when we think about risk. One helpful way is to think about risk in three different buckets. The higher risk bucket is the growth potential bucket. That's money we don't need for the next ten or twenty years. Then we have a mid-range bucket in which we will invest more conservatively. Maybe that's five to ten or fifteen-year money. Then we have our protected bucket, something that has some guarantees, something that we know we can't lose. It's intended to always be there.

Imagine the market suddenly drops 30 percent tomorrow. This might be scary if you don't have something in that protected bucket because the electric company is still knocking on the door. You don't get to tell them, "You know what? Once my stocks have recovered in value, I'm going to catch up on that bill." They won't wait. The property tax collector is there. Some of the things you dreamed about and want to do are still happening. Having a protected bucket can offer options. You might say, "I can take my income from this protected account that isn't exposed to the market fluctuation." The ability to ebb and flow and to get income from the risk or protected buckets can offer greater confidence in retirement.

Imagine being able to truly take advantage of market opportunities. When we think about risk, we also think about opportunity. If we think back to the beginning of COVID, the market dropped very quickly. If you had some portion in that protected bucket, you may have been able to say, "Hey, why don't we take a portion of the protected bucket? Maybe we should buy into the growth bucket, our risk bucket, while share prices are lower." You could then move some money back into the protected bucket to replenish it at the appropriate time. It's commonly suggested that when the market's down, it might be a good time to buy in. Well, that's great, but most retirees don't have large amounts of cash sitting on the side to invest when that opportunity presents itself.

If you look at some of the most successful billionaires, they often buy in very heavily when the market's down. Most of us mere mortals don't have billions of dollars lying around, and we don't have the luxury of saying, "If it takes twenty years to grow, I can wait twenty years." We need it; we're in retirement, but having some risk diversification can give us some available money to potentially take advantage of these opportunities and address our concerns and help ensure we have a steady income, regardless of the market conditions.

Watch for Red Flags

Think back a little bit to some of these more recent market pullbacks. Maybe it's the beginning of COVID, or maybe you think back to 2008 in the housing crisis. We could even return to the dot-com bubble burst, when the Nasdaq-100 sank 78 percent from March 2000 to October 2002.[1] If you think back to those periods and think about how much your portfolio lost and how quickly, and you say, "Boy, at this stage of life, that would be troubling," or, "that would be so concerning," that might be a great indication that your risk is too high.

It's a very simple process, sitting down with a financial professional and talking about these various risks. Having your portfolio analyzed and stress-tested can help answer, "Am I aligned with the risk I'm emotionally comfortable taking?"

---

[1] Will Daniel. Fortune. May 22, 2022. "It's looking a lot like the dot-com crash again. Is the economy headed for an early 2000s-style recession?" https://fortune.com/2022/05/22/why-crypto-tech-stocks-crash-recession-dotcom-bubble

If that answer is no, then the next question can be, "What's the most opportune time to help balance out that risk, to take that bucketed approach, and to help ensure I have my protected money, my mid-term money, and my growth bucket? I can balance these different buckets to help ensure I'm better positioned to help take advantage of opportunities in any market period."

We know having too much money at risk could put you at real risk of losing a large portion of your assets, and that's a big concern for many people. Again, I would challenge you to ask how much risk do you have to take to have a successful retirement? Do you need to take the risk? Some risk can be great because, in good years, you have the potential for better returns, but it's a two-sided coin. It also comes with the potential to lose as much as 20, 30, and 40 percent in those down years. What impact would that have on your retirement?

Balance is Crucial

When we think about investments and financial products, we must consider balancing growth potential, stability, and liquidity. You can typically have two of those, but not all three. For example, if you put your money in a growth bucket, generally, it's pretty liquid—meaning you can cash it out and take that whenever you want—but it's not protected from loss. In most cases, if you want some guarantees that you can't lose some of your money; you don't get much return if you want liquidity. Your money is sitting in a bank account, earning fairly low interest rates. If you want some stability with more growth potential, you tend to give up liquidity. A balanced bucket approach is usually considered a prudent course of action in retirement.

How much should be in each bucket, you ask? That answer is going to be different for everybody. Some people are going to have more in the growth bucket. Some people are going to have more in the stability bucket. This allocation will largely be driven by how large your assets are, your comfort level, and risk tolerance. A customized, balanced approach can help you attain a level of stability in retirement.

CHAPTER 4

Income Dilemma

When we speak with our clients, we discuss the "income dilemma." What does that mean, and why is it important for you to understand?

The income dilemma in retirement is twofold. Many people don't have a definite idea where their income is going to be coming from and likely have not accounted for rising inflation and rising taxation. Maybe you've heard a commercial on TV that says you need $1 million or more. The reality is that some of those big numbers might be encouraging fear and eliciting an emotional reaction. The answers will be very different for different people, but you want to know where your income's coming from, from what account, and in what order. We also must address rising inflation and rising taxation.

When we create a Social Security strategy for couples, we often find one spouse is a higher earner and receives a larger

Social Security benefit, sometimes even twice the size (or more) of their spouse's. If the working spouse were to pass away, they of course want to ensure their spouse continues to be taken care of. One option is to take a reduced pension payout while working so that more is left for their spouse if they were to outlive them.

Remember, most private pensions don't increase with the cost of living. Ten or twenty years down the road, the monthly pension payout will remain the same as it is today. But, added together with Social Security, savings in other vehicles, such as a 401(k), plus required minimum distributions that begin at age seventy-two, it's possible for a couple to have more income in retirement than they ever had while working.

We Can All Get Caught in This Dilemma

The common advice you may have received from Mom, Dad, Grandma, Grandpa, Aunt, Uncle, or somebody else in our life says, "Just stick away every penny you can into that 401(k) because, when you retire, you're going to be a lower tax bracket, so you won't owe much in taxes."

Well, for couples like Tom and Suzanne, that wasn't the case. They're making more money in their seventies than when they were working.

The standard married filing jointly tax deduction in 2022 is $25,100. People over sixty-five get a little bit more, for a total deduction of $27,600.

Tom and Suzanne fell in the most common income tax bracket, filing jointly, at 12 percent. Remember, in 2026, the current tax code expires, 12 percent becomes 15 percent, and their deduction is cut in half. That's a tax increase of 25 percent.

Here's the real dilemma. We know statistically, men don't live as long as women. If Tom passes—maybe he's out on a golf course and trying to drive that ball, and he swings a little too hard and falls over right there on the ninth hole—Suzanne is going to lose the smaller of the two Social Security payouts. Her income goes down, and now she's filing singly, so she gets a significantly smaller deduction.

She goes from a 12 percent to 22 percent income tax rate, an 83 percent increase. She has less income, but the tax bill has nearly doubled. Many people don't consider this dilemma.

These income tax dilemmas can be addressed, but they can't be addressed as effectively once Tom passes away. We're much better off when we meet somebody early in retirement. We can implement strategies to help address this income tax dilemma. A lot of people don't think about this change when one of them passes away, and they lose the benefit of the married filing jointly brackets. Those single brackets are not very favorable and could cause significant increases in taxes, even if your income is lower.

A Simple Strategy

There are dozens and dozens of different tax strategies that we can implement, and they're going to be different for everyone. It's really important to implement tax strategies where appropriate, as they could really impact the longevity of your plan.

The Roth conversion strategy can be effective, especially with the historically low tax brackets that we're in right now. If you look at the tax rates historically, the highest that the top bracket's ever been is 94 percent. In 2022, that top rate is only 37 percent. The last time it went up to 94 percent was the first time in our country's history when we had more debt than GDP, which you can think of that as the country's ability to make income. We had more debt than income as a country. Rates went up to 94 percent, and it took a long, long time to get those back down.

For the second time in history, we have more debt than income. Accounting for a rising tax rate environment and taking advantage of the low tax rates we now have can be an effective tax planning strategy.

Bow hunting has been a long-time passion of mine. One of my favorite weekend activities is to go out for some early morning pheasant hunting with friends.

The kids and I love to try our hand at escape rooms. It's a great chance to test our wits and spend time bonding as a family.

Hunting has taken on added meaning since my son started joining me in the great outdoors. Anthony and I are pictured at left with a pair of turkeys.

There's nothing better than going out and experiencing something new with the kids. Pictured at right is my youngest daughter, Ava, during our trip to Disney World.

We love the sport of water skiing. My kids have entered water skiing competitions across the country. Pictured at left is my daughter, Alyssa, an internationally ranked water skier. In 2021, she took second in the Jr. World Championships.

CHAPTER 5

Tax Planning: Can It Help Me?

A lot of retirees are surprised that they're paying more taxes once they retire.

This is why we want to plan for risk diversification and tax diversification. There are three buckets in our tax system.

Bucket #1—Tax Deferred

This bucket is where a large percentage of Americans' wealth lies. It includes your 401(k)s, 403(b)s, 457s, thrift savings plans, and traditional IRAs. We get the income tax deduction when we put money in, and it can grow tax-deferred, meaning when we take the money out (usually in retirement), we're taxed at the tax rates in effect at that time. Withdrawals before age fifty-nine and a half will be subject to an additional 10 percent federal penalty, too. At seventy-two, if we're not taking money out of these qualified retirement plans, Uncle

Sam forces us to start taking money in the form of required minimum distributions. If we don't take them out, there's a 50 percent tax penalty. It's pretty ugly.

Bucket #2—Taxable

Imagine an investment in a stock or an FDIC-insured CD at the bank: You get a 1099 at the end of the year, and you have to pay taxes every year on any growth. These are examples of the taxable bucket and could include short- or long-term capital gains. For many Americans, this taxation may be lower than ordinary income tax rates.

Bucket #3—Tax-FREE

This is my favorite bucket. That has a nice ring to it: "tax-free." Maybe if you can't fall asleep at night, you can recite that to yourself, "tax-free." It's a nice mantra.

In my experience, many retirees have little tax diversification. All or most of their wealth is in that tax-deferred bucket, and our goal is to help them balance those three buckets. Some of us have been told the narrative that we're all going to be in this tiny tax bracket when we retire, but that's not the case for some of us. Many families and couples we meet are in a higher tax bracket when they consider Social Security, pension, and required minimum distributions. God forbid one spouse in a couple passes away, and now the other is left in a single-filer tax bracket, which is an even higher rate.

More Income = More Taxes

Some retirees find themselves with more income and paying more taxes than they ever did working. A lot of us can't even take an itemized tax return anymore. Maybe you're putting $10 or $20 in a basket at church each week, but you can't write that off anymore because you use the standard deduction. That standard deduction can cause additional taxation for many.

Not having that tax diversification can potentially handcuff you. When you're in retirement, if all of your money is in a tax-deferred bucket, then every time you need to take out a dollar, it's taxed, and you have to take out a little bit more to pay Uncle Sam.

If you need $4,000 a month to supplement your retirement, there's nothing wrong with that. That's why you've saved the money in the first place. But, you might have to actually take out over $5,000 a month to pay Uncle Sam his portion, using up your assets more rapidly by taking this larger percentage out each month or year.

When we have the flexibility of taking some money tax-free, some tax-deferred, and some taxable or implementing a Roth conversion strategy, we have more flexibility and greater control over our tax bill. Instead of Uncle Sam completely controlling the tax bill by potentially pushing us into higher tax brackets, we get some choice as to when and how much we pay in taxes. Controlling when and how you pay taxes can potentially have great benefits, and tax diversification might help you reduce your taxes. I often say there are the mandatory taxes we all have to pay, and then there are the optional taxes we can often eliminate with proper planning.

Tax Strategies: the Earlier, the Better

There are many tax strategies available, but a Roth conversion strategy typically works better if we can meet people earlier in retirement. Why is that? If you come to me at age seventy-two, and you're starting to take required minimum distributions, the tax code says you must take that taxable distribution first before you can do any Roth conversions. If you think about the different tax categories or percentages as buckets, that process starts to fill those buckets up, so we might already be in a higher bucket. That doesn't give us a lot of room to do Roth conversions.

If I'm fortunate enough to meet you earlier in retirement or pre-retirement, you may not have started Social Security and your taxable income may be lower. Maybe all you have is a pension. On paper, you might be in a very low-income tax bracket. We might start to do Roth conversions and take advantage of those lower buckets, the historically lower tax rates we're experiencing now.

That could be a more effective strategy the earlier we meet. We can still implement tax planning strategies in our seventies and later, but we typically can't do as much, and these strategies typically have a smaller impact over the long term. The sooner we get this kind of planning going, the better.

Remember, tax codes change. My best guess is that tax rates are going up, not down. Every year that goes by with lower rates, there's a lost opportunity to do Roth conversions for the maximum tax savings. This trend could hurt your portfolio's longevity. We can implement other strategies as well, but, if timed correctly, a Roth conversion can be an effective strategy for many people.

QCD, DAF, and CRT

I sometimes get complaints from some of our retired clients who say to me, "Tony, I'm putting this money in the basket at church," or, "I'm giving a hundred dollars here and $500 there to various charities, but I can't even deduct it on my taxes." I think a lot of people hear about charitable strategies, and they think, "Boy, I have to be incredibly wealthy to take advantage of this." Fortunately, that's not the case. There are a couple of very simple charitable strategies.

The first one is called a QCD, a qualified charitable distribution. Let's say you're over seventy and a half, and you're giving $500 a year to church. Instead of giving them $10 a week, we can have $500 come right out of your IRA and go to the church. You get to skip income taxes on that distribution, and you reduce your required minimum distribution by that amount for that year.

With this strategy, you're not forced to take out much taxable income. That's a no-brainer. However, if you're donating to any qualified charity when you're seventy and a half or older, there are some limits on how much you can give per year. Still, this is a very simple, and often very effective strategy.

The next strategy is a little bit more detailed: using a donor-advised fund (DAF). Let's assume for a moment, for simple math, that you're giving $2,000 a year to charities. Instead of giving that $2,000 a year so you don't have enough donations to itemize, let's front-load your donations, contributing $20,000 for ten years—or maybe even fifteen years, and putting in $30,000—into a donor-advised fund at once. We get to write a percentage of that off, depending on the type of donation and what your adjusted gross income is.

This can lower your tax bill in the current year!

We still control that account to invest how you see fit. You can still payout that $2,000 a year to the charities but now get a nice deduction upfront. That can help offset or minimize the taxes due on a Roth conversion or potentially allow us to do more Roth conversions without incurring a higher tax bill.

Layering tax strategies together can be important and very effective.

I'll mention one last charitable strategy called a charitable remainder trust (CRT). How many of you reading this have, at one point, owned an asset you wanted to sell—maybe a building, business, stock, or mutual fund—but were hesitant because you didn't want to pay a long-term capital gains bill?

I had a great client who came in with a similar issue. He was a carpenter. When he was twenty years old, he started his business, and it was very successful. He worked hard. His wife was a brilliant doctor.

Between his business and her income, they were considerably high-income earners. In his carpentry business, my client had three other partners younger than him. As he reached his retirement, his partners bought him out of his carpentry business, but they also wanted to buy his building.

Well, when he bought the building, he paid $250,000. This initial payment is what we call the basis. That building now was worth $2 million. That difference meant a capital gain of $1.75 million. If he sold that building in 2022, and his top capital gain rate was 23.8 percent, he'd owe $416,500 in federal capital gains.

In some cases, opening a charitable remainder trust can eliminate the capital gains tax. Rather than someone buying an asset from a person, they instead buy it from the trust.

One of the requirements of a CRT is that it must kick out income to the person who donated it. The minimum is a 5 percent annual withdrawal.

If that withdrawn money isn't needed immediately, it can also be re-invested in other areas. So, if the investment grows at a rate higher than the withdrawal, the annual income will grow each year. Now, that income is taxable, but using a CRT can still result in large gains overall if this strategy is done correctly.

You might be saying, "That's great, Tony. I like that, but we have three beautiful children, and our goal was to leave that $2 million building to the children. This is a great strategy, but in the end, that asset is gone."

In that case, another possibility is to create an irrevocable life insurance trust. We buy a second-to-die life insurance policy—meaning its benefits will only be provided after both you and your spouse pass—that's going to have a guaranteed death benefit of $2.4 million that could pass on to those three beautiful children outside of estate taxes, inheritance taxes, and income tax-free.

Not only would this strategy generate a net $70,000 a year of income, but it also would avoid over $1.5 million in taxes while still passing on $2.4 million to the kids, income tax-free. That's an example of an effective tax planning strategy.

There are dozens of different strategies, but many families we meet with may know only a little about Roth conversions. Many more don't know about these more advanced tax strategies that could possibly have a significant difference in the long run for their finances.

A friend of mine said something funny to me the other day. She said, "Many people think a good tax strategy is hiding money under the mattress!"

That's not the worst idea I've heard lately!

CHAPTER 6

How Do I Manage Healthcare In Retirement?

One of the things I found throughout my career is that sometimes we have to talk about things that aren't comfortable. Today, many retirees have been good savers and are retiring earlier, yet still don't get Medicare benefits until age sixty-five. Often, there's what we call gap coverage—the period we need to find health coverage from retirement age to sixty-five.

Then there's the big dilemma: "When I turn sixty-five, everybody and their brother is calling me. Do I buy a Medicare Advantage plan? Do I buy a Medicare Supplement plan? I'm so confused. There are parts A, B, C, and D. What do I need? How do I sort through this? How do I make sure the plan fits my needs?"

If we fast forward a little bit later in life then there's that period when expenses start to go up because we have more aches, pains, and health concerns.

Then lastly, we can look further down the line to long-term care. Long-term care can create major costs for families and reduce their assets quickly if not planned for properly. How do we sort through all this?

That's when having that dynamic income plan helps. There are many myths out there you may have heard, such as, "You need $1 million to retire," or "Once you retire, you only need 70 to 80 percent of your pre-retirement income." These are myths however, and any concern they bring can be minimized with proper planning and strategy.

Let Me Ask You a Question

How many people want to retire and spend 20 percent less on day one of retirement? I'm guessing that's not going to be many of us. In fact, many retirees enter this early stage of retirement and actually spend more than they had before.

Tom Hegna calls it the go-go stage. You're out doing fun things, living the retirement of your dreams, and checking off bucket list items. Then you hit the second stage in retirement, the slow-go stage. Now your spending tends to cut back.

Maybe your hip or knee hurts. You've done the fun stuff you like to do, and now you want to work on a garden at home or be close to the grandkids, so your expenditures may go down.

Then later in life, you reach the no-go stage when healthcare expenses tend to increase. Having a dynamic plan that addresses these different stages of income needs can be crucial.

In my experience, a lot of people hear about long-term care, and they want to hit the panic button. Not everyone buys long-term care insurance, but for some people, purchasing long-term care insurance might be the best choice for them. With traditional long-term care insurance, there is the potential for rising premiums. Providers can't raise your rates individually, but they can raise everyone's in, say, your age group or your ZIP code. As you can imagine, when you hit eighty and may need this insurance, those rates might can become too high to afford.

Think about it. If you're dealing with a publicly traded insurance company, they can sell this insurance to you in your sixties. Let's say you pay on it for twenty years. It's possible then that the rates go up to point where you either must reduce your benefits or say, "Look, I'm going to have to let this thing go. I'm on a fixed income. I can't afford it anymore." That kind of scenario can be a real advantage for the company. They've collected premiums for twenty years and paid out nothing to you.

For some of us, long-term care insurance is the right answer, but others may want to look at other options. There are numerous ways to address the long-term care dilemma. One is certainly traditional long-term care insurance. But nowadays, there are also some effective alternative products.

Alternative Options

There are alternative products to long-term care insurance such as specific types of life insurance or annuities. You can purchase an additional long-term care benefit, and later in life, if you decide you want to take the money out for long-term care, you can access the surrender value of the product (you won't get a refund of the LTC benefit premiums, but the base product may have a cash surrender value you can access). And if you don't use it, the money passes on to your loved ones.

There are always pros and cons when looking at insurance products, so you want to be very careful. You should understand the details, costs, limitations, and restrictions of a given product. You should also look at its features, the credit-worthiness of the company providing the product, and any time commitments you're taking. These alternative products can be great for some, and some of us can afford to self-insure. Testing that possibility should be a part of your plan.

Some of us might want to lean on legal documents. There are great elder law attorneys who can help with various forms of trusts. Some of these trusts can help protect your assets from long-term care expenditures.

The answer to the long-term care dilemma will be different for everyone, but sticking our heads in the sand and not thinking about it is *not* helpful. A good friend told me, "When you stick your head in the sand, you expose a very large target." I know it's uncomfortable. None of us wants to think about winding up in a nursing home. We all say, "Well, I'll take care of my spouse." The reality is, that's not always possible. Sometimes you physically cannot care for your spouse, or vice versa. Sometimes your health condition is so complex that a home healthcare agency cannot properly support you in your home, and you must stay in a nursing home.

Let's make sure your remaining spouse or family isn't completely wiped out of the money you've worked so hard to save due to unforeseen health problems and a lack of planning.

Review What You Already Have

In a successful Retirement-Ready Roadmap, you're going to review those long-term care policies, or you might already have one of these alternative solutions. In that case, you can review your current situation and ask, "Hey, am I in the right product? Does it have the most effective features and benefits for what I'm trying to accomplish and want to take care of in my retirement?"

There are lots of different details and levers in these policies. Sometimes you alter a few of these details and can significantly reduce your premium and save money. Sometimes you have a policy that's not effective because it doesn't have enough benefits, and you need to make some adjustments. Having a second set of eyes from a comprehensive financial planner or a fiduciary (an advisor who must put your interests first) can make a real difference.

One problem I sometimes see with these types of policies is with insurance agents who can sell long-term care policies but aren't properly licensed or trained to also look at investments and risk diversification. These pieces need to work together. Some of those insurance agents are incredible, but some of them are only looking to sell a product—sometimes in a vacuum.

Having a trusted individual to look at how these pieces work together in a comprehensive plan and address all five areas of your Retirement-Ready Roadmap can help offer you greater financial confidence in retirement.

CHAPTER 7

Family Continuity & Planning

Family is the foundation of our very existence. Are you putting yours at risk when it comes to estate planning?

Generally, one the biggest risks is not having an estate plan. What an estate plan needs to entail will vary for everyone. Some of us may simply need a will, healthcare, or financial power of attorney. A will is a set of instructions telling the court what we want to happen with our assets. Power of attorney is more of a living document. It states, "If I'm unable or unwilling to make my healthcare or financial decisions, I want this person to help me do that." These are documents I believe most of us need to consider.

Some of us are going to need more advanced trust planning. When we think about continuity and continuance, these legal documents become important. But, like long-term care, this kind of planning can be uncomfortable or distressing.

Nobody wants to think about passing away early. Nobody wants to think about what their family will go through dealing with probate or the distribution of an estate after their death. If you've been through that yourself, you understand that it is a very arduous process. The level of difficulty your family will face is very much dependent on how well you plan. It can be a logistical nightmare for them if you don't plan at all, but it can also be a fairly simple process if you do.

There are so many stories about estate planning errors, even from famous stars. In 1998, Sonny Bono passed in a skiing accident and left behind an estate worth $1 million. Because he didn't have a written will, court battles ensued between his one-time wife and singing partner, Cher, and someone who claimed to be Bono's child. A DNA test eventually showed the child was a fraud, but it still took years to sort out who would receive payouts from Bono's estate.[2]

---

[2] Vanessa De La Rosa. ThinkAdvisor. March 20, 2014. "6 tragic celebrity estate plans." https://www.thinkadvisor.com/2014/03/20/6-tragic-celebrity-estate-plans

Lack of Planning Can Equal Family Turmoil

No one wants their family to go through turmoil due to a lack of planning. Simple planning can help protect your spouse or family and minimize the stress that your loved ones go through when you are gone.

Depending on your specific situation, proper estate planning could have a large impact on the tax bill on your estate as well. Depending on the size of your investments and how you're invested, you might use a trust to help accomplish your different goals based on your needs.

Some people need more advanced trust and tax planning to help ensure their family keeps as many hard-earned dollars as possible.

Sometimes I ask people, "What's your largest expense in retirement?" Most people don't know the right answer. For many of us, it's taxes. I haven't met a family yet that says, "Tony, when I pass away, I want to make sure the government's taken care of, and they get most of my assets." Most people don't want that, but that's what could happen if you don't implement tax and estate planning.

Too much of it may end up with Uncle Sam, and that's not what we want. It's not what we need. Some very simple planning can help ensure this doesn't happen.

Some Are More Complicated than Others

There will be some families we work with who require a much more complicated plan. They might need a revocable trust and an irrevocable trust. They may have various types of trusts working together, seeking to accomplish different things.

Some trusts are going to help protect assets from the nursing home; some are designed to help avoid various estate taxes; some will help avoid different generation-skipping taxes. These strategies can be very complex, or they can be pretty simple. A revocable living trust is very common. A revocable living trust is a trust that splits when someone passes, helping to avoid some estate taxes and keep assets out of probate. These also could be very simple but can become very advanced. A mistake I see many people make is avoiding this end-of-life planning, doing nothing, and sticking their heads in the sand.

We don't want you to fall victim to procrastination due to your estate planning anxieties. We want to make sure you're planning for this important part of your Retirement-Ready Roadmap.

Single, Divorced, and Blended Families

This might be the group that needs the strongest estate plan because your goals and wishes can be very, very different. Maybe you're cohabitating with someone, or maybe you're in a silver marriage—a second marriage later in life. There are all kinds of questions that come up in these more complex scenarios. If you are in a second marriage or cohabitating, do you want your money to go to a specific person and their family? Do you want to say, "Hey, while we're together, we want to share expenses, but anything that's left I want to make sure is distributed to my kids and grandkids"? Those can be some very complex and intricate situations to work through.

Also, with second marriages, there's sometimes the concern that if one of the two passes away first, the remaining spouse will change the documents, so everything benefits them and their family. These are some ugly things to think about, but I've worked with retirees long enough to see this happen.

We must help our clients address all these possibilities, plan for them, and ensure they're addressed. There are a lot of great trust and planning strategies that can help deal with these complexities. These strategies will be different for every family, based on what is important to you.

Some people say, "Look, we bought this house together. Whether we're cohabitating or it's a second marriage, I'd like my spouse or my partner to have that for the rest of their life. Then when they pass, I want my half to go to my family and the house to be sold." Or maybe they say, "Once I pass, things are split, and I want my money to go to my family."

There can be very different needs. Another issue we deal with is families that are raising a child with special needs. A special needs trust can be a very effective way to make sure that a child is always taken care of. There's a big dilemma however. If Mom and Dad take care of this child with special needs, what happens when the one or both of them pass away? What happens when we're unable to care for this person anymore? Do we want care to shift to the siblings or another family member? What do we do to protect them?

Typically, that special needs child has some great benefits from the government, healthcare, and sometimes some financial benefits. Inheriting money can disqualify them from receiving the benefits they need and rely on. A special needs trust can be an effective way to say, "I'm going to set aside some money for their care and their needs, and have it structured in a way that it doesn't disqualify them for their benefits." For many families, that's crucial because they don't know who will care for this person. Sometimes the siblings don't want to, or the parents don't want that burden to fall on siblings if they are raising young families. Working through those issues and talking about them with our estate planning attorneys becomes an important part of these families' plans.

Begin the Conversation

My preference when beginning retirement planning is to meet everyone who might be involved in a client's finances. Discussing finances can be a tricky dynamic. It's often much easier to allow your advisor to help start the conversation, especially if anyone is uncomfortable talking about it.

I've been in this industry and working in various parts of the financial world since 2002, but I have focused my practice on retirees and comprehensive financial planning since 2007. I've seen that shifting dynamic firsthand. The retirees I met in 2007 tended to be the baby boomers' parents. That generation didn't talk about money. That was taboo. They did not want their kids to know how much money they had. They didn't want to talk about any of it. As you can imagine, this lack of open communication caused some financial drama and challenges for many families.

Today's baby boomers tend to be much more open with their families about their financial situations and estate planning. They're more dynamic, and they often want to have those conversations. Once we've established a plan, my preference is to have the family members informed: Include the loved ones who will be involved or impacted by your passing and estate and say, "Here's the plan. Here's what we're doing and why. Here's some suggested best steps for when you inherit this to help avoid taxes and to help administer this effectively."

We talked about Grandma and Grandpa earlier. For many of us, what we go through as a child becomes the foundation of how we view money. Maybe you were in a household where Mom and Dad always said, "Money doesn't grow on trees," so you've developed a scarcity mindset.

Maybe you were in a family, where your parents talked about money and investments, and you knew you could work hard and anything was possible financially.

Maybe you're sitting here saying, "Boy, I'm in one of those families that doesn't talk about it. How the heck do I start this?" It starts with a simple conversation. Maybe it's saying, "The way we've addressed our finances in the past isn't effective and I don't think it's working. I want to have an open dialogue about what we have, how our plan works, and how we think it's going to serve you."

I know a lot of people who come in and say, "Hey, Tony, I'm worried about outliving my money." Other couples come in and say, "Tony, I'm worried about my money outliving me. I want to spend it all. In an ideal world, the day I pass away, my checkbook will balance to zero and I will have spent every penny." If you fall into that second group, you may say, "Why in the world should I talk to the kids about it? I want to spend it all anyway."

The hardest part of my job is meeting a couple early in retirement, full of life and vitality, enjoying their retirement and then something tragic happens sooner than we hoped. We want to plan for the worst and hope for the best.

If your goal is to spend all your money, we'll work to create a plan to help you do that. But if something happens too early, we'll also work to help ensure Uncle Sam isn't the biggest beneficiary. We want to make sure everything goes smooth for your loved ones. Even though you wanted to spend it all, my guess is you don't want it all to go to Uncle Sam. You want it to go to your loved ones. This focus and forethought are the foundations of a great estate plan.

My Hope for You

My biggest hope is to give you hope! You might be thinking, "I don't know what to do", and this can cause any of us to be paralyzed in fear. That's no way to live. That's no way to celebrate the forty, fifty, sixty years you spent saving, doing the right thing, possibly forgoing some of the pleasures in the moment to save money and plan for the future.

That's no way to live in retirement—to be paralyzed because you're worried about market risk, inflation, rising taxation, or rising healthcare costs.

One day, you could wake up in your eighties, and you can't plan for the future or take control of your assets in the same way you could earlier, and then you'd ask, "What am I going to do? Am I going to take all this money and bury it with me?" You could miss some great opportunities.

I want you to see that there's a simple, yet effective way to put together a Retirement-Ready Roadmap to help you address all these issues, offering you the potential for greater confidence that you may be able to live the retirement of your dreams.

Consider Tom and Suzanne—we met them in their sixties—and helped them implemented a Social Security strategy. We adjusted their portfolio so it aligned with the level of risk they were comfortable taking. Then we started converting IRAs to Roths, established a trust, and helped them walk through their healthcare concerns. This type of holistic planning has the potential to create additional money that's available for spending or passing on to your loved ones.

Some people come in and say, "Tony, I'm going to eat spaghetti and ramen. I'm going to spend as little as possible because I want to pass on as much as I can to kids and grandkids." If that's your goal, let's set up a plan to help ensure Uncle Sam gets as little as possible. We'll work to leave the kids and grandkids in a good position.

Maybe your ideal outcome is somewhere in between.

CHAPTER 8

How We Can Help You

Our process is very simple. We set up a complimentary meeting with you to create a Retirement-Ready Roadmap.

The sole purpose of this meeting is to understand you better. We talk about the five areas on a Retirement-Ready Roadmap and get a sense of how well you feel you're prepared in those five areas. Are you a 1, or are you a 10? Remember, no 7s are allowed.

Then we start to break everything down more to help understand you. What are your goals, dreams, and desires? What does the word retirement mean to you? What's the why behind your retirement?

When we create a plan for you, we never lose sight of what matters to you. That's always first and foremost, but we also don't lose sight of what we can control.

We've found there are some commonalities in almost everyone's retirement. Most want to make sure family continuity is in their plan and everything will be okay for their spouse and loved ones. They want to make sure their income is accounted for and they have a plan to address concerns of outliving their money. And, they want to make sure they can still do fun, recreational, bucket list stuff. These are some of the why's in most people's retirements: family, income, and recreation. These are the reasons why you saved and worked so hard.

But, we never lose sight that the money is the how, and the money funds the why's. Although the money funds the goals, it's still important to remember the money isn't the entire retirement plan; it's part of it.

We've identified that having a process for your retirement planning that's been tested, adapted, and changed over the years is important. Our process is rooted in our philosophy—how we look at the past and how we look forward with anticipation instead of apprehension. Remember, it's not the direction of the wind but the set of the sail. This discovery process gives us a lot of insight into what's important to you as a family.

If you would like to set up your complimentary discovery appointment, please visit us at:

www.retirementreadyroadmap.com.

In the second complimentary appointment, the design meeting, we'll talk about some high-level ideas, specific planning areas (like the income plan), tax strategies, estate planning concepts, portfolio efficiency, and risk analysis. We'll identify some areas where we think we might be able to help you. This meeting is when most families decide if we're a fit.

Of course, we're certainly not a fit for everybody. Once you determine that we are a fit, we can transfer assets over, like-for-like, without selling anything. We are simply moving from your current custodian to our custodian.

Once transferred, we'll take a deep dive into your finances and our planning strategies. We will address the specifics of investing, tax strategy, and your income plan. We won't change any of your investments without your approval. And, maybe it's not until the second, third, or fourth version of your plan that you give us that approval. We'll keep reworking your plan as we get to know you better.

I can't reiterate enough that you still need more than just a plan. You need to have ongoing planning. You need to be able to make mid-course corrections.

How do we potentially take advantage of different economies, tax laws, and ongoing changes in retirement? These outside factors can change just as your priorities and needs change. We must adapt your plan, so it's an ongoing, living, breathing document throughout your retirement.

My Wish for You

My wish is that you take action. It does not need to be with us. But I suggest you find a good advisor, a fiduciary, who can create a comprehensive retirement plan that can offer you greater financial confidence.

We've found that inaction is often one of the biggest causes of retirement issues. There are so many strategies that we can implement, but some of them are time-sensitive. Some of them are different depending on your age or what chapter you are in within your story. Inaction can be a real disadvantage to your future.

I hope this book has given you some hope, regardless of where you are in the process. Remember, I want you to take action, make your retirement better, and live the retirement of your dreams.

The best way to reach us is at retirementreadyroadmap.com. We also have a podcast called *The Retirement-Ready Show* that we'd love you to tune into. You can get that wherever you like to listen to your podcasts, or you can always reach out to us at 414-409-7226 or by emailing retire@drakeandassociates.net.

The Retirement-Ready Roadmap: Five Steps to a Secure Retirement

Congratulations! You've done it; you've reached retirement. You worked hard and sacrificed and socked away your money into your retirement accounts. Now it's time to enjoy yourself and do things on your terms.

If you are like many retirees, you had an HR representative or advisor who helped or guided you when you were working. They may have suggested you put your money into retirement accounts specifically so you would have money to enjoy in your retirement. Wouldn't it be great if, now that you are retiring, you had someone on your side to help you figure out how to get all that money out in a tax-efficient way too?

That's where we come in. We help people like you figure out which accounts to potentially convert, which accounts to keep, and which accounts may need to be used first because, as they say, "Timing is everything."

Here's what you do next to learn more about the ideas discussed in this book.

Step 1: Download **The Retirement-Ready Roadmap** to see five common potholes retirees tend to fall into when planning retirement and how to potentially avoid them: www.retirementreadyroadmap.com/book-roadmap

Step 2: Listen to a portion of the **Retirement-Ready Podcast** to hear more about what you may need to do in retirement and when: www.retirementreadyroadmap.com/book-podcast

Step 3: Schedule a **Retirement-Ready Discovery Call**, where we get to know your goals and dreams in retirement. *www.drakeandassociates.net*

We look forward to guiding you on the second half of your exciting retirement journey and helping you create your Retirement-Ready Roadmap.

TONY DRAKE, CFP®

Founder & CEO, Drake & Associates, LLC

Tony Drake was born and raised in Milwaukee, Wisconsin. He graduated from Pius XI high school, went on to receive his insurance licenses, CFP® designation, and, finally, a financial planning certificate from DePaul University. Tony is an Investment Advisor Representative and is licensed to manage money in the market. With over twenty years of experience in the financial industry, Tony has served clients from all over the country and specializes in asset preservation, retirement planning, and tax strategies.

In addition to serving his clients, he trains and mentors other financial professionals all over the country. He hosts the Retirement-Ready radio show and podcast. Tony lives in Oconomowoc and has three beautiful children. As a family, they participate in waterskiing tournaments all over the country. They love sports and spending time together. Tony bow hunts, owns wire-haired griffons, and can often be found pheasant hunting with friends.

www.ingramcontent.com/pod-product-compliance
Lightning Source LLC
Chambersburg PA
CBHW052118150726
48002CB00006B/2406